HAMPSHIRE

A portrait in colour

————

BARRY SHURLOCK

COUNTRYSIDE BOOKS

Also by Barry Shurlock
EXPLORE HAMPSHIRE
(With John Holder)
THE SOLENT WAY
THE TEST WAY
DORSET RAMBLES

First Published 1987
© Text Barry Shurlock 1987
© Pictures listed on page 80

COUNTRYSIDE BOOKS
3 CATHERINE ROAD
NEWBURY, BERKSHIRE

ISBN 0 905392 84 1

Produced through MRM (Print Consultants) Ltd., Reading
Typeset by Acorn Bookwork, Salisbury, Wiltshire
Printed and bound in England by Borcombe Printers, Romsey

Contents

Buckler's Hard — Front Cover

The origins of most settlements in Hampshire are lost from the record. The development of the layout of even substantial towns like Fareham is uncertain: was a 'new town' laid out in the Middle Ages or was it a much later creation? There are no such doubts about Buckler's Hard: it was planned in the 1720s by the 2nd Duke of Montagu as a 'shore station' for importing and refining sugar cane from St Lucia and St Vincent in the West Indies.

But the scheme, devised at the time when the South Sea Company was making many rich, was a disaster. Despite having a grant from George I, the duke's men found that the Caribbean islands were defended by French forces and they had to return to Hampshire 'sugar-less'. (Interestingly, a sugar refinery was successfully started in Southampton in 1740.)

Following this unfortunate debacle, plans for the new settlement were scaled down to provide for a loading point for timber from the New Forest and later a celebrated shipyard. A Maritime Museum tells the story of the yard, where a succession of naval vessels was launched in the 18th and early 19th centuries.

The great charm of Buckler's Hard is that it feels as if its 18th century occupants are still there. At any moment you expect them to appear from the cottages which line the main street, or see them at prayer in the tiny chapel which remains.

King Alfred Statue, Winchester — Back Cover

When Sir Hamo Thornycroft sculpted this statue to mark the celebrations in 1901 of the millennary of King Alfred's birth he created an object which has come to symbolise Winchester.

Although the organisers of the elaborate pageant and associated events presented at this time got the date wrong (scholars now believe that the great Saxon leader died in AD 899), they were undoubtedly right to choose Alfred, for he is now known to have created the grid pattern which still dictates the layout of the city. Winchester was the largest of the defended townships or *burhs* created by King Alfred throughout Wessex in the late 9th century.

Introduction

'At no time have I lived more fully than in those
weeks and months spent in Hampshire during each
year of my life.'

Robert Potter, *Hampshire Harvest*, 1977

The purpose of this book is to give a flavour of Hampshire, a county that is so diverse in its landscape and so rich in its literary and historical associations that only a lavishly illustrated encyclopaedia could do it proper justice.

Hampshire has two great assets – its key position between London and the Continent and the waters of its creeks and harbours. Other counties are fortunate to have farming lands as rich as Hampshire's, but none has all the geographical advantages that from the earliest times have given the county its intrinsic importance.

The main centres of the county – Winchester, Southampton and Portsmouth – have at various times played a central role in the history of the nation. The West Saxons chose Winchester as their capital and fused together the petty kingdoms of England from their Hampshire base. Only later did London assume its dominant role.

Hampshire has also been fortunate in its people: William of Wickham, Gilbert White, Jane Austen, William Cobbett, Charles Dickens, Florence Nightingale, Lord Denning, James Callaghan and John Arlott – these are just a few of the many 'Hampshire Hogs' whose careers have enriched the English way of life.

Hampshire is really two counties, divided not so much into 'town and country' but into 'coast and not-coast'. It would still have become a fairly prosperous county without a seaboard, but the advantages of its superb harbours have given it a national importance beyond the reach of other shires. A fortuitous narrowing of the English Channel by the outjutting Cherbourg Peninsula has for centuries made the Solent an obvious landing for anyone crossing from Normandy.

The Romans set up ports at Portchester and Clausentum, near Southampton. When Norman and Plantagenet ruled England and part of France, they often sailed for the French coast from Hampshire. And when France became a long-standing enemy it was at

Southampton and on the Hamble, briefly, and then at Portsmouth that naval ships were built and serviced. A succession of famous national actions, such as Henry V's Agincourt, Nelson's Trafalgar and Eisenhower's D-Day have all started from these shores.

Although Portsmouth was used for Royal Naval actions as recently as 1982, when the Falklands Task Force left for the South Atlantic, it is now Government policy to run down the Naval Base. In the spirit of 'making the best of a bad job', the naval traditions of Portsmouth are being preserved for tourists. The harbour already has Nelson's flagship HMS *Victory* and the famous *Mary Rose*, raised from the sea-bed by archaeologists, and will have the first British iron-clad ever built, HMS *Warrior*. Together with the many museums and other attractions that already exist on both the Portsmouth and Gosport shores, these famous vessels make the area unique.

Perhaps the greatest asset of the Hampshire coast is that its inlets and harbours are remarkably deep at all states of the tide. This is because the deep-cut valleys of such rivers as the Hamble and the Lymington, once tributaries of the great Solent river, were flooded by rising sea levels (which also severed the Isle of Wight from the mainland). Such deep waters were major factors in making Southampton and Portsmouth such large ports ('double tides' at the former were also important). They also help to explain why Hampshire has become so popular with yachtsmen and other 'weekend residents'. Sheltered by the Isle of Wight and provided with the finest back-up facilities in the country, the Solent has become the undisputed capital of the sailing world. Amongst those who have acclaimed it, by word or deed, are Sir Francis Chichester, Chay Blyth, former Prime Minister Edward Heath, Clare Francis, the organisers of the Whitbread Round the World Race and many more.

Solent City, as the coastal fringe is sometimes called, is quite different from that other face of the county, 'Old Hampshire'. This is a land of ancient villages and quaint timber-framed thatched cottages, which have survived because they were solidly founded on chalk and were for centuries part of large estates. Many of these pretty houses are found in the villages strung out along the river banks – the Clatfords, the Candovers, the Wallops and the Worthys.

In general, Hampshire is not a county with great architectural treasures, though it has its fair share of fine farmhouses and handsome manor houses, together with a handful of great mansions. These include Broadlands, Breamore House and Stratfield Saye (all pictured in this volume), Mottisfont Abbey and The Vyne. This famous house, which dates in parts from the mid-16th century, was once owned by a Speaker of the House of Commons.

'Old Hampshire' has always been influenced by its estates and the great county families who held them – the Wallops, the Paulets, the Barings and many others. But until relatively recently, vast areas were also held by the Bishop of Winchester and such foundations as Winchester College and St Cross Hospital, a role that is today perhaps mimicked by City institutions and Middle Eastern potentates. By virtue of its administrative grip on the affairs of parishes, the Church and its allied interests could act like a sort of 'county council'. Alresford, for example, is a 'new town' created in the Middle Ages on the instructions of its lord, the Bishop of Winchester (though the present town is a Georgian rebuild following a fire).

Alresford is just one of a number of small Hampshire towns which are quite unspoilt and a real pleasure to visit – places like Petersfield, Odiham, Whitchurch, Lymington, Bishop's Waltham, Wickham, Ringwood and Overton. These and a large number of other places (notably Winchester) are protected as Conservation Areas and are the parts of 'Old Hampshire' which it is the policy of the County Council to preserve. Further growth in the county is to be confined mainly to the south coast, Andover, Basingstoke and the north-east of the county, where dramatic developments have taken place in the last 20 years.

The communities of Hampshire have, of course, been strongly affected by local influences, particularly the presence of the sea and the nature of the soil: the contrasts between those places which stand on chalk and clay are particularly marked. A glance at the map will show that the claylands of the north-east corner (the modern districts of Hart, Rushmoor and Basingstoke) and the lands of the Hampshire Basin in the south of the county are much more densely settled than elsewhere. This contrast has always existed and modern growth has accentuated it.

The county's claims to belong to the twentieth century are to be found in such places as Portsmouth, Havant, Southampton, Eastleigh, Basingstoke and Farnborough. Here are found the 'household names' such as Vosper's, Pirelli, Ford, IBM (also at Winchester and Hursley) – and many others – who help to make Hampshire an area of low unemployment. The county's largest cities also contain its major educational establishments, Southampton University and Portsmouth Polytechnic.

The rest of Hampshire is relatively sparsely populated: less than 20 per cent of its million and a half people live on the chalk. This is where agribusinessmen work the 'prairies' of central and northern Hampshire to give some of the highest yields in the country. The soil is thin but modern methods allow nutrients to be replaced each year in a style of agriculture that one farmer once described as 'close to hydroponics'. It is good business, but unfortunately it is impoverishing the landscape.

In the north of the county the chalk lands rise to great heights in a range of hills that overlook the western limits of the Thames Basin. Such viewpoints as Inkpen Beacon, Beacon Hill and Watership Down (made famous by Richard Adams's book and Martin Rosen's film) are amongst the highest on the chalk; further north it plunges beneath the clays, gravels and sands of South Berkshire.

The valleys of Hampshire's chalk streams were once valued for their meadows and mills. In more recent times they have been cherished by countrymen and 'fanatical' fishermen. A paucity of public footpaths and a plethora of 'keep out' signs, though resented by many, have preserved these areas in a semi-wild state. Controlled public access to some reserves is possible at places such as Winnall Moors, near Winchester, and Titchfield Marshes. These are administered by the Hampshire County Recreation Department and the Hampshire and Isle of Wight Naturalists' Trust, respectively, bodies which are helping to preserve the county's wildlife for a caring audience.

These and many other 'heritage-saving' schemes are perhaps the most characteristic features of Hampshire today and will surely be seen in future years as enlightened moves by people determined to make the most of the county's treasures.

'If the writer should at all appear to have induced any of his readers to pay a more ready attention to the wonders of the creation, too frequently overlooked as common occurrences; or if he should have lent an helping hand towards the enlargement of the boundaries of historical and topographical knowledge . . . his purpose will be fully answered.'

Gilbert White, *Natural History and Antiquities of Selborne*, 1789

Winchester Cathedral

Winchester City

One of the successful balancing tricks performed by planners in recent years has been to keep Winchester a pleasant place to live in and yet allow it to share the 'boom town' atmosphere of modern Hampshire. Much of this success must be due to the fact that as a city it has retained that natural drawing power that all capitals must have. This made it the Saxon capital of England and an important city in Norman times, but its modern vitality must surely be due to the one thing that once almost choked its streets, the motor car. Winchester is a natural 'day out' for people from a large number of places within easy reach.

Much of the main street of the city, which runs between the Westgate and the Broadway, is now a pedestrian precinct. At the top is the Great Hall, the one remaining building of the medieval castle that once stood on the West Hill. Alongside stand the modern law courts where the Assizes are held. Below, in the centre of the pedestrian area, is the distinctive Queen Anne building that was once the city's guildhall, now occupied by Lloyds Bank. Nearby are the Butter Cross, the timbered facade of God Begot House (formerly held by an ancient manor within the city), The Square and City Museum.

The great width of the Broadway is a relatively modern feature, dating from the 18th century. It includes the flamboyant Victorian Guildhall, the banqueting hall at St John's House and Abbey House.

I came to this place in hopes of meeting with a Library, but was disappointed. The High Street is as quiet as a lamb.

John Keats, 1819

The Hospital of St Cross

The Wayfarer's Dole is a custom which refuses to die at the Hospital of St Cross. Ask for it at the Porter's Lodge and you will be given a piece of bread and a glass of beer.

It is a relic from the Middle Ages, when the roads thronged with poor men and pilgrims and charitable institutions were set up by the church to serve them. Despite its ancient buildings, St Cross is still a 'working charity', for it is a retirement home for 24 men, who either wear black or red gowns.

The Black Brothers are supported by the original foundation of the hospital, created by Bishop Henry of Blois in 1136, while the Red Brothers depend on the later foundation of Cardinal Henry Beaufort, who in 1446 formed the Order of Noble Poverty.

The brothers live in the rooms on the west side of the quadrangle of the hospital. Opposite is the Tudor range which once served as an infirmary. It communicates with the great chapel, which exhibits a variety of architectural styles reflecting the long period over which it was built.

Although set up with the best of intentions, St Cross has often served the needs of its master more than those of its brothers. Anthony Trollope's classic novel *The Warden*, published in 1855, was inspired by Salisbury but is said to have been closely modelled on the Winchester hospital at a time when the self-enriching activities of Francis North, Earl of Guilford, were a public scandal.

I will be no backbiter, whisperer, maker or favourer
of those who make false reports; no causer of anger,
hatred, discord, envy, reproach, strife or quarrel, but
I will endeavour to promote unity, peace and concord
within its walls.

Extract from the oath sworn at St Cross
by new brothers

The River Itchen

Central and northern Hampshire is a land of 'valley dwellers'. Some thrive by the Meon, others adore the Test, while there are those who are happiest by the Itchen.

These great chalk streams have in relatively recent times become renowned throughout the world for their fly fishing, but for centuries they were valued for their constant waters, which were a boon for those who owned mills.

Winchester in particular owed no small part of its wealth and power to the fact that the Itchen powered a dozen or more mills within or near the city. Six of these were held by the bishop, whilst City Mill – still standing in its 18th century form – was the most valuable asset of the Abbess of Wherwell. Alresford, Alton, Romsey, Whitchurch – all these and many other places depended on the waters of their rivers.

The sites of several hundred mills are known in Hampshire, the oldest at Fullerton, on the Test, where archaeologists have discovered the remains of a Roman mill. But the rivers also served other important industries, including fulling (a process for finishing cloth), brewing, tanning and papermaking.

The Itchen seeps out of the ground near Cheriton and quickly becomes a sizeable stream. It runs via a chain of pretty villages to Winchester, where it slips almost unseen through the city. The picture shows a stretch of the river above Easton, which is depicted in Janet Marsh's bestselling *Nature Diary*, published in 1979 in a forlorn effort to stall the building of the M3 motorway across these lovely water meadows.

Most pure and piercing the aire of this Shire: and none in England hath more plenty of clear and fresh rivulets of troutful water

Thomas Fuller,
The Worthies of England (Hampshire), 1662

The Watercress Line

With the exception of a spur to Alton, the central area of Hampshire in 1973 was without a railway. This followed closure of the Alton–Winchester line as part of the 'Beeching cuts'. But Hampshire steam enthusiasts (for the line had not been electrified) would not be quelled by bureaucracy and within four years were running trains again on what is popularly called 'The Watercress Line'.

Volunteers have now reopened the entire track between Alresford and Alton via Ropley (whose station is shown in the picture), providing an hourly service in the summer. For the traveller, this has restored the link with British Rail services. For the romanticist, it has kept alive the unique experience of speeding through the countryside by steam train.

As its nickname suggests, 'The Watercress Line' provided a vital link with markets in London and elsewhere for locally grown watercress. The spring water that bubbles out of the Hampshire chalk is ideal for growing the plant: it is wonderfully clean and its temperature is a constant $51/2°F$. The railway enabled fresh-cut cress, which was once the only greenstuff available in the winter, to be rushed to the markets in a saleable condition. Hampshire Watercress Ltd, based in Alresford, has played a major role in developing this cottage industry into a modern business.

Elsewhere in Hampshire the coming of the railway allowed other perishable goods to be rushed to market, especially strawberries and crabs and lobsters.

Watercress is reckoned to be a sure-fire cure for a hangover

John Bevan, *A Taste of Alresford*, 1985

Waller's Ash, near Winchester

This isolated cottage to the north of Winchester stands close to the spot where Sir William Waller, the Parliamentarian General, is reputed to have rested under a tree after the Battle of Cheriton in 1644, before marching on Winchester. When Waller's Ash Tunnel nearby was dug for the London–Southampton railway in the late 1830s, a number of swords and other weapons were unearthed. These may be the relics of the skirmish between Waller's men and Royalists which took place here when Winchester finally fell, eighteen months after the Cheriton fight.

Waller's Ash Cottage is typical of so many of the thatched brick-and-flint cottages which are the traditional dwellings of Hampshire. The native style of thatch is termed 'long straw', as the wheat stalks lie more or less along the slope of the roof. Today, this has almost entirely been displaced by the more durable 'wheat reed' method, in which the cut ends of the stalks form the surface of the roof. The older method can always be recognised by the hazel strapping which was required to hold down the straw at the eaves.

To the right of the cottage can be seen the Lunway, an ancient trackway from Old Sarum, which leads to the Lunways Inn on the Winchester–Basingstoke road. An earlier route once ran further to the south, skirting the southern boundary of the Worthy Down racecourse, which was patronised during the summer by Winchester and London Society. Beyond the Lunways Inn the track meets a drove road leading to Alresford.

Perhaps the most plausible explanation of the Lunway was that it was an early attempt to find an easy passage of the rivers Test and Itchen, avoiding the heavy forests and steep hills that guarded Winchester.

C. Cochrane, *The Lost Roads of Wessex*, 1968

Breamore House

Hampshire's western boundary runs round a tooth-shaped piece of land which juts out between Wiltshire and Dorset in the vicinity of Fordingbridge. Breamore House stands beside the river Avon and guards this strange 'peninsula', which dates only from boundary changes made towards the end of the last century.

The house was built for William Dodington in 1583 in the shape of an 'E', like so many other Elizabethan houses. Its early history was marked by tragedy: Dodington threw himself off a London church steeple, while his grandson murdered his mother in a fit of pique and was himself hanged for the deed.

In 1748 Breamore House was sold to Court Physician Sir Edward Hulse, who had inherited the position earned by his father at the court of his countryman, William of Orange. Breamore House still remains in the family, though much of its fabric was rebuilt after a disastrous fire of 1856. The most impressive room is the Great Hall, which has the dimensions of four cubes joined end on end.

During the last war Breamore House was occupied by the headquarters staff of US General Patton. It is now open to the public and amongst the attractions to be seen are an impressive Countryside Museum with large displays of old tools and farm machinery.

Breamore church is a particularly rare example of a Saxon ecclesiastical building. It dates from about AD 980.

Here the Covenant becomes manifest to thee
Translation of the Anglo-Saxon
inscription in Breamore church

Yachting in the West Solent

Hampshire's southern coast was almost purpose-built for the relatively modern sport of sailing. Its deep-water havens have made it second to none as a centre for yachtsmen. Once it was possible to sail up to Hamble or Lymington in the presence of only a few boats, but today a berth at a crowded marina or 'marina village' is the best that can be expected.

The 'headquarters' of sailing is on the Isle of Wight, at the Royal Yacht Squadron, Cowes. But Hampshire's coast has its fair share of Royal Clubs and is at the very centre of the sailing world. Each autumn at the Southampton International Boat Show, designers show off their latest vessels and yachtsmen gather to plan the next year.

The line-up of yachting celebrities who have been based in Hampshire is amazing: Clare Francis at Lymington, Sir Francis Chichester at Beaulieu, Chay Blyth and Edward Heath at Hamble, Sir Alec Rose at Portsmouth, and many others. All these have discovered that the semi-enclosed waters of the Solent and Spithead and their numerous inlets and creeks are ideal for 'messing about in boats'.

To soak up some of the atmosphere, the landlubber has only to 'sit and stare' at Hamble or Eling or Lymington or even take the little ferry that runs in the summer months from Keyhaven to Hurst Castle. From here there is a good view of the Milford-on-Sea coastline shown in this picture.

One ship sails east, one ship sails west
By the self-same wind that blows.
It isn't the gales but the set of the sails
Which determines the way that she goes.
Traditional

Lymington

A harbour full of luxury yachts, a street market as lively as Whitechapel's and a beautiful coastline that is a 19th century industrial wasteland: these are some of the features that make Lymington a fascinating place to visit.

Situated on a rather remote corner of Hampshire's shores and insulated from Southampton and The Waterside by the New Forest, Lymington has become a major centre for sailing. The yachting scene is centred on the Royal Lymington Yacht Club, whose modern premises command a grandstand view of the harbour. But a refreshing dose of ozone can be found at the foot of Quay Hill, shown here, where vessels of 500 tons once offloaded their goods and took on salt.

The ancient industry of extracting salt from sea water was the main source of the town's income until the early decades of the last century, when it was overtaken by the salt mines of Cheshire. Remains of the salt pans and boiling houses which once lined the coast between Lymington and Keyhaven can still be seen from the local paths that form part of the Solent Way, a long-distance footpath that runs between Milford-on-Sea and Emsworth.

A steamer service operates between Lymington and Yarmouth on the Isle of Wight. A spur from the London–Bournemouth railway line runs between Brockenhurst and the ferry pier.

Having knocked about in boats for the last 59 years, I am quite happy to prop up the Royal Lymington Yacht Club bar, be fed 'Bloody Marys' and talk boats to anyone who cares to indulge in this delicious pastime.

Alastair Easton, yacht broker, quoted in
J. Chitty, *The River is Within Us:
A Maritime History of Lymington*, 1983

The New Forest

Any tendency to think of conservation as 'modern' is bound to suffer from a visit to the New Forest. For this vast area of south-west Hampshire owes its survival to the complex 'conservation' laws which the Normans originally drew up to protect their hunting reserves. Minor disputes were heard in the Verderers' Court, which still sits regularly in Lyndhurst, the capital of the forest.

It was in the New Forest that William the Conqueror's son, Rufus, was killed in 1100 by an arrow, though to this day it is not known whether he was murdered or killed by accident. A stone marks the spot at which he fell, near Cadnam.

The New Forest is particularly known for its special breed of ponies, which roam the wastes and woodlands. They are carefully controlled by their owners, the commoners, who round up the animals for regular sales held at a site near Beaulieu Road Station.

One of the most popular places to visit in the forest is the Rhinefield Ornamental Drive with its Tall Trees Walk, a long avenue of such giants as Douglas Fir, Redwood and Wellingtonia.

Some of the people particularly linked with the forest include 'Brusher' Mills, the legendary snake catcher, Sir Arthur Conan Doyle, buried at Minstead, and Heywood Sumner, the gentleman archaeologist who showed that the forest is littered with the remains of Roman pottery kilns.

The history of the forest for at least nine centuries has been dominated by the conflicting aspirations of the Crown — first in deer conservation and the construction of a landed estate for political and economic motives, later in the exploitation, growth and harvesting of timber — and of the commoners in using the Forest to support their livestock and provide other natural produce.

Colin Tubbs, *A Natural History of the New Forest*, 1986

The Cradle of Cricket

Broadhalfpenny Down, near Hambledon, in east Hampshire is widely regarded as the birthplace of cricket. It was here and at Windmill Down nearby that the famous Hambledon Club played for a glorious half-century or so after its formation in about 1750. This fortuitous event brought together a remarkable group of men who put cricket on the map: they did not invent the game, nor was their club the first to be formed, but they were a major influence in making it the sport that it became.

John Nyren's *The Cricketers of My Time*, published in 1833, set down memories of these golden years, culminating in the defeat by the village club of the All-England side in June 1777. The hero of the match was James Aylward, a farmer's son, who scored 167 runs, one more than England's first innings total.

In more recent times another son of Hampshire, the broadcaster John Arlott, who for many years lived at Alresford, has made an equally distinguished contribution to the game, albeit with pen and microphone. His warm Basingstoke accent was for many years synonymous with the lazy days of summer.

Village cricket is still one of the delights of the English countryside and in Hampshire is still regularly played at many places, including Hursley, Longparish, Petersfield, Lyndhurst (shown here), Cadnam, Easton, Burghclere and Hartley Wintney, which has one of the oldest greens in England. The Hampshire Cricket Club, which was not formed until 1863, plays at Southampton, Portsmouth, Bournemouth (now in Dorset) and Basingstoke.

A man who is essentially stupid will not make a fine cricketer; neither will he who is not essentially active.

John Nyren, 1833

Beaulieu and the National Motor Museum

Throughout Hampshire the Dissolution of the Monasteries brought old lands to new owners. Beaulieu (literally 'beautiful place'), founded by King John, had for more than three hundred years been worked by Cistercian monks when it was acquired in 1538 by the Lord Chancellor, Thomas Wriothesley, later created Earl of Southampton. Of all those who gained from the Dissolution, he probably profited more than anyone else.

The Beaulieu estate has been passed down to his descendants ever since, though it only became a 'permanent home' in the 1860s, after Henry Montague-Douglas-Scott was given it as a wedding present. The Scots Baronial Palace House he fashioned around the monastic gatehouse dates from this period.

The present owner, the 3rd Baron Montagu of Beaulieu, is shown opposite with his family in a Silver Ghost Rolls-Royce, one of the star exhibits in the National Motor Museum which he created at Beaulieu. He was one of the first owners of stately homes to realise that the only way to retain his great estate was to open it to tourists. This shrewd response to changing times has, amongst other things, earned him the job of chairman of English Heritage, the government quango that manages castles and other national treasures.

Beaulieu is situated on the edge of the New Forest in a most beautiful part of Hampshire. It offers a wide variety of activities: some will be attracted by the Museum of Monastic Life or the ruins of the abbey or the archives of the National Motor Museum. Others will prefer the monorail or a trip on a London bus.

The English kings intended its abbots to be public figures, yet it is hard to find any one of the personalities of this story attractive, though some are colourful enough.

Dom F. Hockey, *Beaulieu: King John's Abbey*, 1976

The Beaulieu River

The Hampshire streams which flow south to the sea were once the tributaries of a great Solent river which carried their waters, and those of some Dorset rivers, to the English Channel. A rising sea level destroyed the Solent river and flooded the valleys of Hampshire's streams. Thus, like the Lymington and Hamble rivers, the Beaulieu river became short, deep and tidal. But unlike these other streams it is still almost deserted, for it is privately owned. Its mysterious wooded banks, which are best appreciated by walking, are typical of the appearance of much of the original Solent shore.

On the left bank below Buckler's Hard stands Exbury House, famed for its fabulous display of rhododendrons early in the summer. Hundreds of unique hybrids have been bred at the gardens, which were created between the wars by the banker Lionel de Rothschild.

At the estuary of the river, the lonely marshy shores of Lower Exbury and Inchmery show a face of the Solent which is rarely seen. Gull Island, which guards the estuary (it is a broken-off chunk of Need's Oar Point) is of national importance for its colonies of breeding birds, especially its Little Terns.

A rich bird life is also a feature of the shores of Lepe Point further west, where a Country Park provides excellent facilities for visitors.

Of all the Solent creeks and harbours, Beaulieu river
is undoubtedly the most beautiful.
K. Adlard Coles, *Creeks and Harbours of the
Solent*, 8th ed., 1972

The Bargate, Southampton

If ever there was a symbol which is instantly recognisable it is Southampton's Bargate. The streets of Above Bar and Below Bar still echo the 'two worlds' of the city, for the Bargate was the northern gateway into the medieval town, where almost all Southampton was contained until the last century. Substantial remains of the ancient town still stand, including the Wool House (used by the monks from Beaulieu and now a Maritime Museum), the Merchants' Hall, the Norman House and much else.

There is also another side to old Southampton, which has caused great excitement amongst antiquarians in recent years. Excavations in the St Mary's district on the west bank of the river Itchen are revealing an hitherto 'lost' Saxon settlement which was probably the largest town of its time in the country. Called *Hamtun* or *Hamwic*, it subsequently gave its name to the medieval port of Southampton, which was built to the south-west.

Today Southampton's role as a regional and industrial centre within Hampshire is only rivalled by Portsmouth (though Basingstoke is rising fast in the north). Amongst Southampton's greatest public assets is its common, which lies half a mile to the north of the Civic Centre and has a surprisingly rich wildlife. It is almost half the size of Central Park, New York.

Fyrst Barre Gate by north and well embatelid. In the upper part of this gate is *domus civica*: and undernethe is the toun prison.

Edward VI, 1552

Southampton Docks

The way that yachtsmen clamour for berths on marinas shows that men who sail the sea will go to great trouble to get what they need. Owners of ocean-going vessels are no different, and so it was that the shoreline of Southampton, with its deep waters and 'double tides', was extensively refashioned to provide the facilities required for a great port.

Until the 1950s, when civil aviation mushroomed, Southampton was the 'Gateway to the Empire' and the home port of such great liners as the *Queen Mary* and *Queen Elizabeth*. It was also from Southampton that the *Titanic* set sail in 1912.

The extent of Southampton's dockside today is vast by comparison with earlier ages. The oldest part (excluding the Saxon port on the Itchen) is that immediately below the Bargate, where the Town Quay still stands. Until land reclamations of the present century the shoreline to the west of the town curved round in a great bay that stretched from the West Quay almost as far as the present Civic Centre.

During the Middle Ages the quayside was kept busy with trade with France, largely involving exports of wool and imports of wine. By the 16th century Southampton had declined and been overshadowed by the ports of Bristol and London, partly as a result of piracy in the English Channel. It was not until the last century that the port regained a position of importance, when the Eastern Docks were excavated. Land reclamation enabled the docks to be greatly extended to the west in the late 1920s and again in the late 1960s, when the container port, shown opposite, was built.

It would be impossible to say where Southampton itself really began, though I should like to think that the true boundary is that corner of East Park where there is a memorial to the lost engineers of the *Titanic* . . .

J. B. Priestley, *English Journey*, 1937

The Waterside, Southampton

Digging for bait as a boy at dusk I once encountered a very curious situation. Amongst the dark mud on my fork were bright specks of light that flashed intermittently. Had I, I wondered, come across a dump of chemical waste, or even the remains of an atomic bomb? The real explanation was much more prosaic, for minute phosphorescent worms are just one of the multitude of surprises found on the Solent foreshore!

Those who enjoy beachcombing can spend hours sifting the shells, stones and jetsam of the Hampshire coast. In several places, particularly at Barton-on-Sea, sharks' teeth and other fossils are washed up in quantity, whilst the local shells provide plenty to ponder. A common find is the quahog, a species of clam with a bright violet mark inside its shell. It is a native of North America and was probably introduced to the Solent via the kitchens of liners.

This picture shows one of the oil tankers which are familiar sights in the Solent. By far the largest local oil installation is at Fawley, on the west side of Southampton Water (called The Waterside). 'Fossilised' in the vast complex of pipes and tanks is the original 670-acre site, which was opened in 1921 to supply fuel oil to ships and to produce bitumen.

This British venture quickly fell into American hands and it was the Esso Petroleum Company which in the early 1950s greatly expanded the site to become the largest refinery in the British Isles. Pipelines now send most of its products to London (including Heathrow and Gatwick airports) and the Midlands.

The value of dry cargo passing through the docks has been overshadowed by the value of the oil passing through the Fawley oil refinery.

Adrian Rance, *Southampton: An Illustrated History*, 1986

Royal Victoria Country Park, Netley

Parks are generally made by keeping the developers at bay. This one was made by demolishing one of the grandest hospitals ever to have been constructed.

At the behest of Queen Victoria, who spent much of her time at Osborne House on the facing shore of the Isle of Wight, the Royal Victoria Military Hospital was planned during the Crimean War but was finished too late to be of any use to the wounded. The huge edifice, 1,404 feet in length, was penetrated by daunting corridors that were wide enough to take a car (and may have done so when the Americans commandeered it in the Second World War!). Its 'sunless' design was fiercely contested by one of Hampshire's famous daughters, Florence Nightingale (named after the Italian city where she happened to be born).

Despite its drawbacks, the great military hospital served men from all parts of the British Empire, particularly during the Boer War and the First World War. The sick and wounded were brought to the doors of the hospital via its pier, or its own branch railway line.

The former chapel of the hospital, shown opposite, is all that was left standing when the 'Royal Vic' was demolished in 1966. It has now been converted into a Park Centre and holds a permanent exhibition of the history of the site.

Elsewhere in Hampshire, in the Haslar area of Gosport, stands the Royal Naval Hospital, a pioneering establishment completed almost a century before the Royal Victoria and still thriving.

'In the year 1878 I took my degree of Doctor of Medicine of the University of London, and proceeded to Netley to go through the course prescribed for surgeons in the Army.'

Dr Watson reminiscing in
A. Conan Doyle's *A Study in Scarlet*, 1887

Portchester Castle

Almost all of Hampshire's Roman remains are underground. The most remarkable exception is Portchester Castle, which stands at the head of Portsmouth Harbour. It has somehow survived for 1700 years and is the finest remaining Roman fortress in northern Europe. In recent years it has been excavated by a team led by one of Hampshire's distinguished sons, Professor Barry Cunliffe.

It was probably built at a time when Roman Britain faced attacks from Germanic peoples and a string of forts was constructed from Wight to the Wash. One of the commanders who held the Channel for Rome was Carausius, who declared himself an independent Emperor of Britain between AD 286 and 293. He was murdered by his second-in-command, Allectus, who after three years was defeated by Imperial forces at a battle somewhere in north Hampshire.

Portchester served as a castle long after the end of the Roman period and only fell into disuse in the middle of the 15th century. One of its grand occupants was Henry V, who stayed here in 1415 before embarking from Southampton for Agincourt. Hereafter, the focus of settlement around Portsmouth Harbour moved to the present site of HM Naval Base, close to the harbour entrance.

The church in the south-east corner of the castle site was built in the early 12th century for a priory of Augustinian canons, who within a decade or two had moved to Southwick nearby, where the community survived until the Dissolution.

The location of Portchester in Portsmouth Harbour was the key to its importance, being the most secure base west of Dover, accessible from central southern England and a convenient point of departure for Normandy.

Barry Cunliffe and Julian Mumby,
Excavations at Portchester Castle, IV, 1985

HMS *Victory*, Portsmouth

HM Naval Base Portsmouth (known to most as 'the dockyard') and its surroundings are gradually acquiring a gigantic open-air museum of naval history. It started with HMS *Victory*, Nelson's flagship at Trafalgar, which was restored and opened to view in the 1920s. Then came the RN Museum. Now there is also the *Mary Rose*, the Tudor warship miraculously excavated from the silt of Spithead, and at Gosport the RN Submarine Museum, with HMS *Alliance* and the very first submersible put into commission, *Holland I*. Soon they will be joined at Portsmouth by the first armoured battleship to be built in Britain, HMS *Warrior*, which was launched in 1860.

The importance of Hampshire's harbours in the defence of the realm can hardly be overstated. Nelson's defeat of the combined French and Spanish fleets at Trafalgar in 1805 was just one episode in a long history of threats from across the Channel. One of the most devastating incidents occurred in 1338 when a French fleet crept onto Portsea's shores, slaughtered a large number of men, women and children and set fire to wooden houses clustered around the south-western tip of the island.

Hampshire's naval connections have had an influence beyond its shores and have imparted a salty tang to some of its most tucked-away places. At Old Alresford, cannon captured from the French in 1782 still stand on the terrace of Admiral Rodney's House, which is open to the public.

'I am a dead man, Hardy. I am going fast: it will be all over with me soon. Come nearer to me. Pray let my dear Lady Hamilton have my hair, and all other things belonging to me.'

Nelson, reported by his surgeon William Beatty in *The Death of Lord Nelson*, 1807, reprinted 1985

Portsmouth Harbour

The great mass of water that rushes in and out of Portsmouth Harbour twice a day keeps scoured a deep channel which helped to persuade Henry VII in 1495 that this was the best place to set up a dockyard for his royal fleet. Portsmouth also had the advantage that it was easily reached from London and gave quick access to the Channel via Spithead.

Henry VIII greatly expanded the dockyard and set off a pattern of patchy growth that continued until modern times. In 1830 the first of the specialist establishments, HMS *Excellent*, was created to train gunners, initially from a hulk in the harbour and then from Whale Island (most of which had been reclaimed by hand). A torpedo establishment, HMS *Vernon*, broke away from the gunners nearly fifty years later, and its example has been followed by the many other specialist branches that modern naval warfare requires.

Old pictures of the harbour often show the string of convict hulks that were moored in its upper reaches. In these cramped quarters, many thousands of people spent their last night in Britain, before being transported to the Colonies. Nearly 200 years ago the first boatload of convict settlers left Spithead for Australia.

During the last century the dockyard was protected from attack from the sea by building a great ring of forts around the harbour, several of which are now open to view. Perhaps the most intriguing of these is Spit Bank Fort, which stands in open sea two miles from the shore. It can be visited during the summer months.

For much of the 15th century, the Hamble River had been preferred for laying up royal ships, and Henry VII might have founded his dockyard there had not the depth of water been greater at Portsmouth.

Jonathan Coad, *Historic Architecture of HM Naval Base Portsmouth: 1700–1850*, 1981

Old Portsmouth and the 'Hot Walls'

When the Falklands Task Force sailed from Portsmouth Harbour in April 1982 it rekindled a warring spirit that had many times echoed between the 'hot walls' at Sallyport and Fort Blockhouse.

It was not long before the horrors of war were brought home to many local families, particularly by the sinking of guided-missile destroyer HMS *Sheffield* a month later, but for a while Portsmuthians were elated by the need to defeat an enemy.

Two years later a memorial was unveiled to the 130 seafarers from the Royal Navy, Royal Marines, Royal Fleet Auxiliary and Merchant Navy who lost their lives in the conflict. It stands at Old Portsmouth, where sailors first started to set sail from Portsea after the Roman harbour at Portchester became silted-up.

The medieval harbour founded in the 12th century is now called The Camber and is still used by a few fishing vessels. It is overlooked by the chapel originally built in about 1180 by the canons of Southwick Priory, which became Portsmouth Cathedral in 1927 when the city obtained its own diocese.

Old Portsmouth became notorious in the 18th century for its bars and brothels and it still has something of the atmosphere that earned it the name 'Spice Island'. Nearby is the High Street with its coaching inns, where Nelson and other naval officers stayed before sailing to *their* wars.

So large is the naval force dedicated to restoring British sovereignty in the remote Falklands Islands that there is little left of the Royal Navy in the home ports.

The News, Portsmouth, April 1982

Southsea and the D-Day Museum

The development of Southsea as a seaside resort owes much to the officers and others who came to settle here in the last century. They liked its fresh open aspect, its facilities for bathing and the sight of soldiers from Southsea Castle drilling on the common!

Southsea Castle was one of a chain of forts built around the coast by Henry VIII in the middle of the 16th century to provide protection against a possible French attack. Others were built locally at Calshot, Hurst, Netley, Cowes and Yarmouth.

Alongside Southsea Castle stands one of the most recent additions to the seafront, the D-Day Museum, which was opened in June 1984 to mark the 40th anniversary of the liberation of Europe. Said to have been designed in a weekend (and yet it has won several awards), the museum was built around an amazing embroidery which depicts the major events of D-Day and its aftermath. Its 34 panels stretch over a distance of 272 feet, which is 41 feet more than the famous Bayeux tapestry.

The Hampshire coast played a key role in the D-Day operation, which was controlled by General Eisenhower from Southwick House, near Portsmouth. Now occupied by HMS *Dryad*, the navigation school, it still contains the Map Room used in the invasion (the D-Day Museum shows a replica of the operations board). On this critical day in June 1944, the Solent harbours were packed with a large part of the flotilla of boats and men which crossed to Normandy.

'Okay, we'll go!'
Allegedly, General Eisenhower's order to
commence the D-Day landings, 5th June, 1944

Windsurfing at Hayling Island

When 12-year-old Peter Chilvers started 'messing about' with a primitive sailboard on Hayling Island in 1958 he could hardly have imagined the outcome. This simple invention has created a multi-million pound industry and has given fun to many thousands.

By coincidence, the sailboard was invented in the place which has become the mecca of windsurfing in the UK. Experts say that Hayling Island offers a variety of conditions suitable for windsurfers of all abilities: the novice can 'learn to stand' in the protected waters off Northney, whilst the dab-hand can use the sea-front, which is especially popular when the winds rise above Force 4.

A highlight of the year is the Hayling Island Marathon, when windsurfers compete in a round-the-island race. The record is held by Malcolm Oliver, who completed the 20-mile circuit in 1 hour 6 minutes.

Peter Chilvers, like many inventors, did not obtain his priority without a struggle. Following the first commercial production of a sailboard in the USA in 1970, a court case (in which Mr Chilvers's mother and others attested to his youthful enterprise) was needed to challenge patents taken out by the Americans.

So skilled are modern surfer-athletes that one of them broke the world speed sailing record in 1986. This now stands at almost 45 mph (38.86 knots)!

Have you heard the catchphrase, 'Hayling is like Hawaii'? Whether it's a slight exaggeration or inspired hype, the slogan describes what is probably the best known English coastal boardsailing site in the world.

Jeremy Evans, *Boards*, 1986

Folk dancing
at Queen Elizabeth Country Park

Although the annual 'revels' that many villages used to hold have long died out, there is today a strong interest in reviving folk events. In Hampshire alone there are about twenty teams of folk dancers, all of them formed since the Second World War. The oldest group is the Winchester Morris Men, who started to dance in 1953. The Winchester Folk Festival has now become an annual event and this year a team from Southampton, calling themselves 'King John', were voted the top English side at the Sidmouth International Folk Festival.

The team shown here at the Queen Elizabeth Country Park, near Petersfield, dance under the extraordinary name of the 'Knockhundred Shuttle Clog Dancers'. They have recreated dances that were once performed in the north-west of England and demonstrate the fact that folk dancing is now no longer tied to localities. In Hampshire the old dances had died out by the last century, with the exception of the 'begging' dances such as May Day routines and Mummers performances, which helped to relieve the awful poverty of the times. Gypsies in the New Forest and elsewhere were the last to keep alive a native tradition of dancing, which only died out in recent years.

'Social dancing' was taught in Hampshire villages until the First World War. On the wedding day of the Duchess of York in 1986, a rather special five-hand reel recalled at her home village of Dummer, near Basingstoke, was recreated by 'Hampshire Garland' and danced under the gaze of television cameras.

Please to see a fine garland,
Made early in the morning.
The First of May is Garland Day,
Please to see a fine garland.

Traditional verse, once said in the
Test Valley at Chilbolton

The Gilbert White Museum, Selborne

Gilbert White's *Natural History of Selborne*, first published in 1789, was an instant success and has been read and 'dipped into' ever since. It is the record of a man who lived the idyllic life of a country clergyman, yet maintained a critical and lively intellectual interest. He was reluctant to publish the letters which make up the book and only went ahead after seventeen years' deliberation.

He was born in the Hampshire village of Selborne, where his grandfather was vicar, but he did not live there until the age of ten, when his father, a barrister, purchased 'The Wakes' (called after a family of that name). He went to school in Basingstoke for three years and then proceeded to Oriel College, Oxford, where he was later elected to a lifelong fellowship. Virtually all of his working years were spent as a local curate in Hampshire, mainly at Farringdon, but also at Newton Valence and finally at Selborne (where he had also served briefly earlier in his life).

Selborne is still full of reminders of Gilbert White, particularly the zig-zag path and the steep hanger which he often mentioned. His simple gravestone, the church he served and the great yew he measured are still there. 'The Wakes' (the view opposite is from the rear) has become the Gilbert White Museum and also contains exhibits on the Antarctic explorer Lawrence Oates and his uncle, African naturalist Frank Oates.

> . . . all nature is so full that that district produces the most variety that is most examined.
>
> Gilbert White, *The Natural History and Antiquities of Selborne*, 1789

Jane Austen's House, Chawton

If as lively a person as Jane Austen had lived for long in a town or large city it is likely that her social life would have been so full that her great novels would never have been written. *Pride and Prejudice* dates from her time at Steventon, the tiny village to the east of Whitchurch where she was born, but her most productive period was undoubtedly at Chawton, near Alton, where she set up home with her mother, sister and a relative in the summer of 1809. This followed a long period when the family lived at various addresses in Bath and also in Southampton.

The church at Steventon where her cleric father served for many years still stands. So, too, does the manor house in the delightful village of Ibthorpe, a few miles north of Andover, where she often visited family friends, the Lloyds. The house at Winchester where she died and her grave in the cathedral can also still be seen. But the most vivid reminder of this great novelist is at Chawton Cottage. Here can be seen the rooms as they were when Jane sat in the parlour working on the books that record her telling observations of the middle class she knew. There is no better way of stepping into Hampshire in the early 19th century than to read the books penned at Chawton.

Throughout her work, we sense Jane's steady belief that it is possible for human beings, however fallible, to build an ordered, loving society.

Anne-Marie Edwards,
In the Steps of Jane Austen, 1979

Beacon Hill and the 'Hampshire Highlands'

Portsdown Hill looks over Portsmouth, St Catherine's Hill beckons Wintonians, while Danebury, with its ghosts of Iron Age man, gazes benignly over the Test Valley. In North Hampshire the great 'chalk mountain' is Beacon Hill, which lures scores of scramblers up from the A34. It is part of that steep escarpment that separates north-west Hampshire from the Kennet Valley and the lowlands that lead eventually to London and the North Sea. This is the natural northern boundary of the county, but the quirks of history have mixed in bits of Berkshire from the north, whilst Wiltshire manages to intrude from the west.

The hill shares its name with several others in the south, presumably recording the fact that it was here that bonfires were lit to transmit urgent messages in times of crisis, such as the appearance off the south coast of the Spanish Armada in 1588. The later pre-electricity 'telegraphs', which used various sytems of semaphore, ran elsewhere in the county, connecting Whitehall with the naval establishments at Portsmouth and Plymouth.

Facing Beacon Hill on the other side of the A34 is Ladle Hill, and beyond that Watership Down, which gave its name to Richard Adams' bestseller. The combine harvester in this picture is a reminder that much of North Hampshire is rich farming country. But the hills (called the 'Hampshire Highlands' by the naturalist G. A. B. Dewar) rise to such heights that they are good only for sheep.

I'm looking forward to a nice doe and a litter of
kittens in my burrow. Lots of little Bigwigs, Hazel!
Think of that, and tremble!

The hopes of Bigwig, a principal character in
Richard Adams' *Watership Down*, 1972

Bere Mill, Whitchurch

The highest reaches of Hampshire's chalk streams are often waterbournes or lavants, i.e. they run dry towards the end of the winter and stay dry until the chalk has been 'filled up' by the rains of spring. Lower down, however, they are as reliable as the tides and were once of enormous importance as a source of power. Several hundred sites of corn mills are known in the county and a few are still working: notably at Headley, near Bordon, at Eling (a tide mill) and at Botley (out of use, but expected to be recommissioned). Many more have been converted to fine houses, like Isington Mill, home of the late Viscount Montgomery of Alamein.

Water power was once vital for weaving and fulling and one of the few silk mills still in business in the country (though now powered by electricity) can be visited at Whitchurch. One of its prime products is legal silk, which is wholly appropriate for the birthplace and home of Lord Denning, Master of the Rolls 1962–82.

Further upstream stands Bere Mill, pictured here, which was the first mill to be held by the papermaker Henry Portal, who took up residence in 1712. The clear, unfailing waters on the Test enabled this well-connected Huguenot emigré to found a business which endures to the present day and has made paper for the Bank of England since 1724. The works are now situated upstream at Laverstoke and Overton.

Henry Portal learned his trade as a papermaker at the mouth of the river Itchen, at South Stoneham Mill, near Southampton, which was run by the White Paper Makers' Company of England.

> Portals are now providing paper for bank-notes of no less than 101 separate Governments and Banks of Issue throughout the five continents – manufactured in the largest banknote paper mill in the world.
>
> Sir Francis Portal, *Portals*, 1962

Longparish and the Test Valley

The Test Valley between Stockbridge and Whitchurch is one of the finest stretches of countryside in England. To those who know it well, the names of the villages bring back memories of drowsy summer days fishing for trout amidst the green luxuriance of a well-watered Hampshire vale. Longstock, Leckford, Wherwell and Longparish are villages which are a joy to visit. They are, in fact, small settlements in one long garden, for the owners of this part of Hampshire lavish great care in preserving their patch. The river banks are mown, the thatched roofs are immaculately repaired, and natural beauty of the area is cherished.

Longparish itself must, as its name suggests, be one of the longest villages in Hampshire. Several hamlets are contained within its three miles, including Middleton (site of a deserted medieval village), where the church shown opposite is located. This contains many memorials to the local squires, the Hawkers, one of whom was army pilot Major Lanoe Hawker VC, DSO, RFC, who died during the First World War, aged 25. A stained glass window erected to his memory is unusual for depicting the airmen of the day and the primitive field bases from which they flew.

The church also contains a memorial to the celebrated Lt-Col Peter Hawker, who fought under Wellington, but is best-known for his huntin' and fishin' exploits at Longparish and elsewhere. He was also an accomplished musician and was well-acquainted with the London opera scene.

1840: Dec 7th: Left Longparish and went, for a change of air from the pestilential vapours of that low water-meadow country, to Keyhaven [near Lymington].

Extract from
The Diary of Colonel Peter Hawker, 1893

Wherwell

One of the many links between Hampshire and the New World is to be found in this pretty Test-side village. The river and state of Delaware are named after Thomas West, 12th Lord de la Warr and the first Governor of Virginia, who owned Wherwell Priory. This fine estate stands beside the church and was acquired at the Dissolution by one of Thomas's ancestors, the 9th baron, (who oddly enough had publicly declared himself against the closure of the monasteries).

Wherwell Abbey was a Benedictine nunnery founded in the 10th century by a Saxon queen, Elfrida, after the death of her husband Edgar, the first King of All England. She is said to have performed this pious act in penance for her complicity in the murder of her first husband (and later of her stepson), Hampshire nobleman Ethelwold. The deed took place during a hunting escapade in Harewood Forest, a couple of miles to the north of the village, at a marked spot which is still called Deadman's Plack.

Wherwell is also renowned for the legend of the cockatrice, a beast whose eyes were the classical equivalent of the laser beam – one glance meant instant death. Said to have had the wings of a fowl, the tail of the dragon and the head of a cock, this fearsome concoction was hatched by a toad sitting on a duck's egg in a dark cellar in the village, according to medieval chroniclers. Possessed of an appetite for human flesh, the cockatrice was an awful nuisance and was only eventually killed by the Star Wars strategy of lowering a mirror into the creature's den.

Wherwell Abbey owned twenty-nine *hagae* [town properties] in Winchester in the early eleventh century.

Winchester in the Early Middle Ages,
Martin Biddle (ed.), 1976

Broadlands House, Romsey

Broadlands is the nearest that modern Hampshire has to a palace. The tradition of royalty visiting this great house is due to the close relationships between the British Royal Family and its former owner, the late Lord Louis Mountbatten of Burma, but its grandeur alone fits it for this role. The Queen and Prince Philip came here after their wedding in 1947, and so did the Prince and Princess of Wales in 1981.

Royal connections with great houses are, of course, not new: former monarchs might stay at Basing House, near Basingstoke, or bring their retinue to quite modest houses, such as Elvetham Hall, near Fleet, or Grove House, near Nursling. At other times they might hold court at Southwick Priory or stay at Winchester, in the castle or in the bishop's residence, Wolvesey Palace.

Broadlands was opened to the public in 1979 and within two months had been pitchforked into the headlines by the tragic assassination in Ireland of its owner, Lord Mountbatten. His grave can be seen nearby in Romsey Abbey, the great nuns' church which miraculously survived the Dissolution in 1539. Part of its lands formed the original Broadlands estate, though the present house dates only from the 18th century. It was built on its fine site beside the river Test by Henry Holland, who added to the work of his father-in-law, 'Capability' Brown, to create a home for one of the ancestors of the Victorian Prime Minister, Lord Palmerston, who lived there. He often spent seven or eight hours in the saddle travelling back to Hampshire after the end of Parliamentary business on Friday afternoon.

'Nothing can be more comfortable than this House. It is magnificent when we have company, and when alone it seems to be only a cottage in a beautiful garden.'

Emily Lamb, Palmerston's wife, quoted by
John Miller, *An Englishman's Home*, 1985

Basingstoke

A directory entry for Basingstoke in the middle of the last century reads: 'The Town is well built, and has several good streets lined with neat houses, shops, inns and taverns.' Many people who visited it before the 1950s would have been able to recognise this description of a place that still retained at least some of its country airs. But since that time it has been changed utterly: the tiny central core of Old Basingstoke is now contained within a great ring road and a penumbra of industrial estates.

Some of the most interesting of the surviving buildings are the former Corn Market, now the Haymarket Theatre, and the remains of the Lesser Market, both in Wote Street. Near the rail station are the remains of the Holy Ghost Chapel, which dates from the 13th century, and the Guild Chapel of the Holy Trinity, built in 1524 by the owner of The Vyne, Lord Sandys.

The story of Basingstoke is told in the Willis Museum, which is housed in the former Town Hall, seen opposite. Its exhibits show that Basingstoke has long been a minor industrial centre, giving birth to at least two well-known brand names – Milwards the shoemakers and Burberry, the waterproof coat.

During the First World War the firm of Thorneycroft produced thousands of lorries for use by the military. The drug company Eli Lilly has been in Basingstoke since the 1930s and the computer manufacturers IBM now occupy several key sites in the town.

Basingstoke is modern, and proud of it.
Brian Vesey-Fitzgerald, *Hampshire and the Isle of Wight*, 1949

Basing House and the Civil War

To the east of Basingstoke stands the small village of Old Basing and the remains of a mansion whose ruination was one of the great stories of the Civil War. It was the home of John Paulet, 5th Marquis of Winchester, whose ancestor William Paulet had acquired a great fortune during the Reformation.

Basing House was a Royalist stronghold during the Civil War and held out against repeated sieges for two years. It was eventually taken by storm by the New Model Army, led by Oliver Cromwell himself, who burned it to the ground in 1645. One of the people taken prisoner was the architect Inigo Jones.

The family fortunes of the Paulets did not immediately revive after the Restoration but restyled Dukes of Bolton they later played a prominent part in the affairs of the county, living at Hackwood Park a few miles to the south-west of Old Basing.

Basing House had long had a tradition of loyalty to the Crown when Paulets inherited it in the 15th century. It was the most important of the fifty-five manors which are recorded in the Domesday Book as being held by the Norman aristocrat, Hugh de Port. The position of his castle is probably marked by a surviving motte and bailey earthwork called 'Oliver's Battery'.

The Sealed Knot shown here re-enact the scenes of the Civil War, often at Basing House, but in this case elsewhere in Hampshire. The ruins, which are open to the public in season, have been extensively excavated and are managed by the Hampshire County Recreation Department.

'By my troth, if my Lord Treasurer were but a young man, I could find it in my heart to have him for a husband before any man in England.'

Attributed to Elizabeth I, referring to the 1st Marquis of Winchester during a visit to Basing House in 1560

The Basingstoke Canal

The lure of the London markets persuaded entrepreneurs in the late 18th century that there was money to be made by linking Basingstoke with the Thames. The major trade was reckoned to be timber and corn 'up' and coal 'down'.

'Canal mania' was, of course, a feature of the times and Hampshire had already acquired the Itchen Navigation to link Winchester with Southampton. In the same year that the Basingstoke Canal opened, the Andover canal to Redbridge (it was never completed to Southampton) was also opened. Neither venture was commercially successful, though the Basingstoke Canal endured longer, from 1794 to 1901, when it carried the last commercial traffic to the town.

The canal reached London via Odiham, Woking and Woodham, where it joined the Wey Navigation. Its engineers managed to reach the county boundary, near Ash, with the use of only one lock (there were 28 in Surrey) and took the bold decision to tunnel through a hill at Greywell, thereby saving a circuitous route of nearly 38 miles. The tunnel twice collapsed and even today continues to cause trouble, as canal restorers argue with nature conservationists on the value of the old tunnel as a roost for bats.

A familiar sight on the canal above Greywell is the *John Pinkerton* water-bus, which takes its name from the man who built the canal and is owned by the Surrey and Hampshire Canal Society. Their members have restored much of the old waterway and its towpath in association with the local authorities.

The completion of the Basingstoke Canal heralded a new era in canal building. It was the first of the so-called agricultural waterways.

P. A. L. Vine, *London's Lost Route to Basingstoke*, 1968

Stratfield Saye House

One of Hampshire's great figures, the 1st Duke of Wellington, was an Irishman by birth, though he belonged to an English family and was educated in this country. His association with Hampshire was purely accidental. At the age of nearly 50, when his military career was over, he took as his country home Stratfield Saye House, which stands near Hartley Wespall in the north-east corner of the county. It was the nation's gift for his victory at Waterloo and he chose this particular estate mainly for its farms: he was never persuaded to replace the relatively modest house with anything grander.

After Waterloo, Wellington turned to politics and twice acted as Prime Minister. During the agricultural riots that swept through the countryside in 1830, when he was Lord Lieutenant of Hampshire, he gained the contempt of the mob by taking an uncompromising stand against the plight of the ordinary man.

Wellington was a practical man who would surely have loved the gadgetry of our century. When asked by Queen Victoria how the sparrows could be removed from the trees enclosed by the great glass pavilion at the 1851 Great Exhibition, he replied laconically: 'Sparrowhawks, Ma'am.'

A prize exhibit at Stratfield Saye House, which in season is open to the public, is the great bronze carriage which carried the duke's remains at his State Funeral in 1852. In the grounds is the grave of Copenhagen, the charger which he rode for 'the entire day' at the Battle of Waterloo.

All the business of war, and indeed all the business of
life, is to endeavour to find out what you don't know
from what you do . . .
Wellington, *The Penguin Dictionary of
Quotations*, 1960

Aldershot Camp

In the middle of the last century both Queen Victoria and Prince Albert took a strong personal interest in two major military projects in Hampshire. One was the Royal Victoria Hospital at Netley (see p. 40) and the other was Aldershot Camp. The War Office confirmed the decision to proceed with a huge new military training camp in April 1854, only a few days after the start of the Crimean War.

Within a remarkably short time the population of the small village of Aldershot had increased twentyfold to 16,000 and a vast area of 'useless' heathland had been compulsorily purchased from commoners and others. The soldiers originally lived in tents, then in wooden huts and finally in red-brick barrack blocks. Most of the earliest buildings, including a Royal Pavilion, have now gone and been replaced by modern buildings. The Aldershot Military Museum and Visitors' Centre, which has excellent displays, occupies the last of the remaining Victorian barrack blocks.

Amongst the corps which have museums in and around the camp are the Queen Alexandra Royal Army Nursing Corps, the Airborne Forces, the Royal Army Medical Corps and the Royal Corps of Transport. Every two years the public have a chance to see the troops in action at the Aldershot Army Display.

The town's most profitable activity was that of satisfying the army's thirst for alcohol.
John Walters, *Aldershot Review*, 1970

Acknowledgements

The choice of pictures for this book is a personal one, but I am grateful to my wife, Liz, and to my publisher, Nicholas Battle, for help in making the final selection. Some photographs were taken specially for the book, whilst others are reproduced with the kind permission of their copyright owners, who are listed below. I am especially grateful to John Barton and his 'family of photographers' and to Ian Swann of the Hampshire County Recreation Department, whose extensive collection of slides enabled Nicholas Battle to persuade me that a 'Portrait in Colour' of the county should be compiled.

Thanks are also due to several specialists, all Hampshire residents, who kindly helped me to fill gaps in my knowledge: Malcolm Isaac, Managing Director of Hampshire Watercress Limited; Roy Dommett, an authority on folk dancing; and international race director Steve Schrier of Pro-Team, who told me about windsurfing.

Barry Shurlock

The copyrights of the pictures belong to the following individuals and institutions:

Front Cover – National Motor Museum, Beaulieu
Back Cover – Barry Shurlock

Barry Shurlock pages 9, 11, 13, 15, 19, 25, 35, 57, 61, 63, 65 and 71; Mid Hants Railway plc 17; Anne-Louise Barton 21; Southern Tourist Board 23; Terry Heathcote 27; Mike Edwards 29; National Motor Museum 31; Phil Colebourn 33; Associated British Ports 37; Roger Haddock 39 and 67; Hampshire Recreation Department 41, 45, 55, 73 and 75; Jeremy Barton 43 and 69; John Barton 47 and 59; Portsmouth City Council 49 and 51; Kier Francis 53; Duke of Wellington 77; *Soldier* The British Army Magazine 79.